P9-CCT-157

Kansas City, MO Public Library
0000180278699

First Facts®

OUR GOVERNMENT

THE U.S. SUPREME COURT

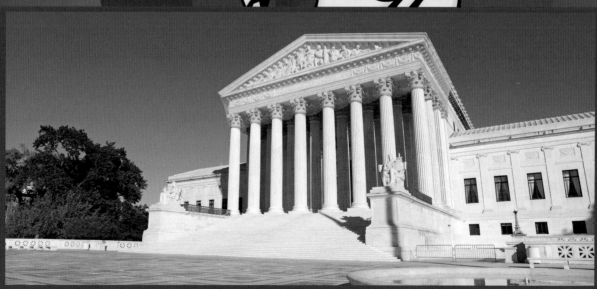

BY ELLA CANE

CAPSTONE PRESS
a capstone imprint

First Facts are published by Capstone Press,
1710 Roe Crest Drive, North Mankato, Minnesota 56003
www.capstonepub.com

Copyright © 2014 by Capstone Press, a Capstone imprint. All rights reserved. No part of this
publication may be reproduced in whole or in part, or stored in a retrieval system, or transmitted in
any form or by any means, electronic, mechanical, photocopying, recording, or otherwise, without
written permission of the publisher.

Library of Congress Cataloging-in-Publication Data
Cane, Ella, author.
The U.S. Supreme Court / by Ella Cane.
     pages cm. — (First facts : our government)
Includes bibliographical references and index.
Summary: "Informative, engaging text and vivid photos introduce readers to the U.S. Supreme
Court"— Provided by publisher.
ISBN 978-1-4765-4203-4 (library binding)
ISBN 978-1-4765-5147-0 (paperback)
ISBN 978-1-4765-6000-7 (eBook PDF)
1. United States. Supreme Court—Juvenile literature. I. Title. II. Title: United States
Supreme Court.
KF8742.C275 2014
347.73'26—dc23   2013034221

Editorial Credits
Shelly Lyons, editor; Kyle Grenz, designer; Wanda Winch, media researcher;
Kathy McColley, production specialist

Photo Credits
AP Images: Dana Verkouteren, 11; Collection of the Supreme Court of the United States, cover
(middle), 17, 19 (all); Corbis: Reuters/Art Lien, 15; Getty Images: Alex Wong, 13; Newscom:
Photoshot/Xinhua/Zhang Jun, 21; North Wind Picture Archives, 9; Shutterstock: Anatoly
Tiplyashin, cover (top), Gary Blakeley, 1 (bottom), 5, Olga Bogatyrenko, cover (back), Sign N
Symbol Production, cover (left), 1 (top)

Printed in the United States of America in North Mankato, Minnesota.
092013   007771CGS14

TABLE OF CONTENTS

CHAPTER 1

MAKING DECISIONS

Have you ever made a decision about rules? Then you have done something that happens in the U.S. Supreme Court time and again.

The U.S. Supreme Court is part of the judicial branch of the U.S. government. The Supreme Court building is in the nation's capital of Washington, D.C.

The Supreme Court building in Washington, D.C.

CHAPTER 2

BRANCHES OF THE U.S. GOVERNMENT

The judicial branch is one of three parts of the U.S. government. The other parts are the legislative branch and the executive branch. The legislative branch writes and passes the nation's laws. The executive branch makes sure laws are being followed.

In the judicial branch, there are many **courts**. The Supreme Court is the highest court. The judicial branch explains the **Constitution** and makes decisions on laws.

court—a place where a judge or judges decide cases about laws
Constitution—the written system of laws in the United States; it states the rights of people and the powers of government

FEDERAL GOVERNMENT

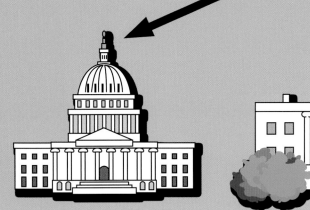
The U.S. Capitol

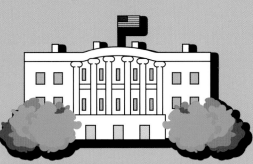
The White House

The Supreme Court

LEGISLATIVE

EXECUTIVE

JUDICIAL

CONGRESS

PRESIDENT

SUPREME COURT

SENATE

HOUSE OF REPRESENTATIVES

VICE PRESIDENT

7

CHAPTER 3

A CASE GOES TO COURT

To decide if a law has been broken, people take a **case** to court. A local or state court makes a **ruling** on a case. People can ask to have that ruling looked at by another court. The Supreme Court reviews cases that were first decided by other courts. Sometimes people ask the Supreme Court to review their case.

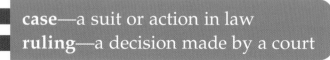

case—a suit or action in law
ruling—a decision made by a court

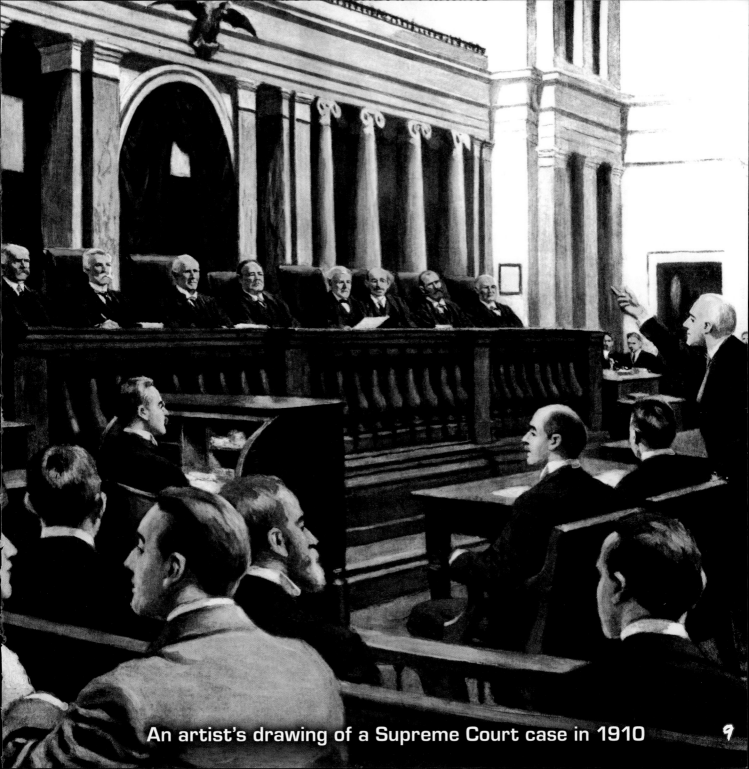
An artist's drawing of a Supreme Court case in 1910

The **justices** review cases to decide whether or not a **federal** law was broken. Federal laws must follow the U.S. Constitution. Justices study the Constitution to make a decision. They also consider decisions made on past cases. Then the justices vote to make a decision.

justice—a judge on the Supreme Court
federal—having to do with the U.S. government

About 10,000 cases are submitted to the Supreme Court each year. From those only about 100 to 150 cases are heard.

11

CHAPTER 4

COURT IS IN SESSION

A **term** of the U.S. Supreme Court begins on the first Monday in October. A term lasts one year. The Court takes **recess** at the end of June. It begins again on the first Monday in October. During summer, justices continue to read cases and prepare for the upcoming term.

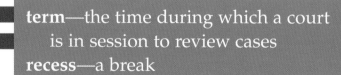

term—the time during which a court is in session to review cases
recess—a break

Supreme Court Justice Sonia Sotomayor

CHAPTER 5

WHAT HAPPENS IN COURT

In most courts **lawyers** ask people questions to explain a case. A judge or **jury** listens to people talk about the case. The judge or jury then makes a decision. In the Supreme Court, only lawyers talk to the justices about a case. Justices ask the lawyers questions to get more information. No jury is used.

lawyer—a person who is trained to advise people about the law

jury—a group of people that decides if a person is guilty of a crime

An artist's drawing of lawyers presenting
a case to the Supreme Court in 2013

CHAPTER 6

THE JUSTICES DECIDE

Justices meet in private to talk about a case. Then they vote on a ruling. At least five of the nine justices must agree with the ruling. One justice writes down the court's decision. Justices also may write about why they do not agree with the ruling. The Supreme Court's decision is final.

FACT Because the number of justices on the Supreme Court is uneven, there can never be a tie.

The justices' private meeting room

CHAPTER 7

HOW MANY JUSTICES?

The first Supreme Court met in 1789. At that time there were just five justices and a chief justice. Today nine justices serve on the Supreme Court. Justices serve until they decide to leave, are asked to leave, or die. Then the president of the United States **appoints** a new justice. The **Senate** votes to approve the president's choice for a new justice.

appoint—to choose someone for a job
Senate—one of the two parts of Congress that makes laws

Five different U.S. presidents appointed the nine Supreme Court justices serving as of 2013. These justices are:

Justice Samuel A. Alito, Jr.

Justice Stephen G. Breyer

Justice Ruth Bader Ginsburg

Justice Elena Kagan

Justice Anthony M. Kennedy

Chief Justice John G. Roberts, Jr.

Justice Antonin Scalia

Justice Sonia Sotomayor

Justice Clarence Thomas

CHAPTER 8

THE CHIEF JUSTICE

The leader of the Supreme Court is the chief justice. Although the chief justice is the leader, he or she gets just one vote on a case, like the other justices. The chief justice **presides** over **arguments** in the Supreme Court. He or she also usually decides which justice writes down the court's decision on each case.

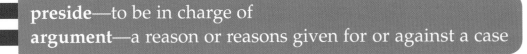

preside—to be in charge of
argument—a reason or reasons given for or against a case

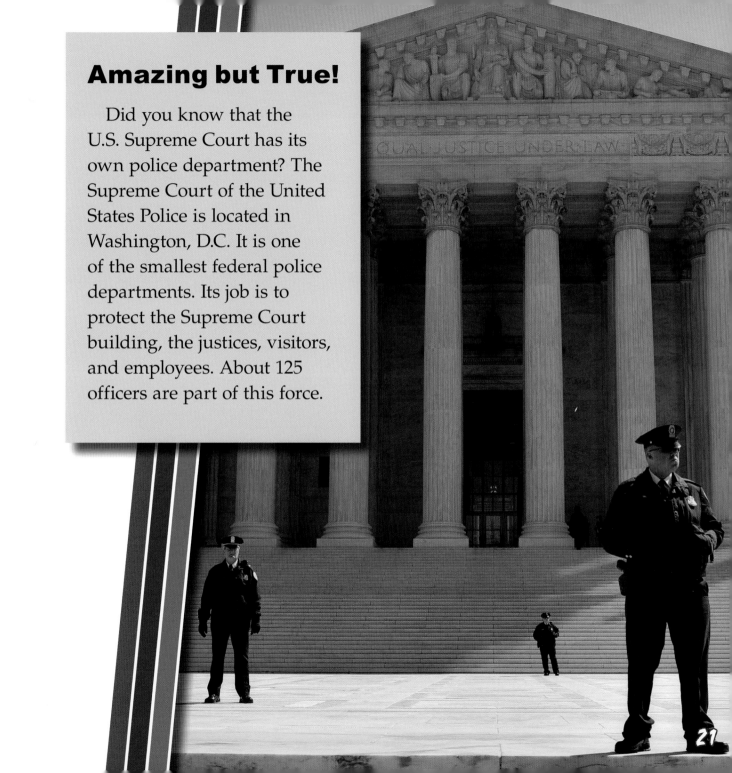

Amazing but True!

Did you know that the U.S. Supreme Court has its own police department? The Supreme Court of the United States Police is located in Washington, D.C. It is one of the smallest federal police departments. Its job is to protect the Supreme Court building, the justices, visitors, and employees. About 125 officers are part of this force.

GLOSSARY

appoint (uh-POINT)—to choose someone for a job

argument (ARE-gyu-ment)—a reason or reasons given for or against a case

case (KAYS)—a suit or action in law

Constitution (kahn-stuh-TOO-shun)—the written system of laws in the United States; it states the rights of the people and the power of government

court (KORT)—a place where a judge or judges decide cases about laws

federal (FED-ur-uhl)—having to do with the U.S. government

jury (JU-ree)—a group of people that decides if a person is guilty of a crime

justice (JU-stiss)—a judge on the Supreme Court

lawyer (LAW-yur)—a person who is trained to advise people about the law

preside (pri-ZYD)—to be in charge of

recess (REE-sess)—a break

ruling (ROO-ling)—a decision made by a court

Senate (SEN-it)—one of the two parts of Congress that makes laws

term (TURM)—the time during which a court is in session to review cases

READ MORE

Jakubiak, David J. *What Does a Supreme Court Justice Do?* How Our Government Works. New York: PowerKids Press, 2010.

Nelson, Drew. *Meet the Supreme Court.* A Guide to Your Government. New York: Gareth Stevens Pub., 2013.

Suen, Anastasia. *The U.S. Supreme Court.* American Symbols. Minneapolis: Picture Window Books, 2009.

INTERNET SITES

FactHound offers a safe, fun way to find Internet sites related to this book. All of the sites on FactHound have been researched by our staff.

Here's all you do:

Visit *www.facthound.com*

Type in this code: 9781476542034

Super-cool stuff! Check out projects, games and lots more at **www.capstonekids.com**

23

INDEX

CRITICAL THINKING USING THE COMMON CORE

1. Congress votes to approve the president's choice for a Supreme Court justice. What are some of the reasons why they have that power? (Key Ideas and Details)
2. The diagram on page 7 explains the three branches of the U.S. government. Who is part of the executive branch? (Key Ideas and Details)